ESSENTIALS OF

ASSERTIVE BEHAVIOR

Shyam Bhatawdekar

Dr Kalpana Bhatawdekar

Essentials of
Assertive Behavior

Books by Shyam Bhatawdekar and Dr Kalpana Bhatawdekar

1. *HSoftware* (Human Software) (The *Only* Key to Higher Effectiveness)
2. Sensitive Stories of Corporate World (Management Case Studies)
3. Classic Management Games, Exercises, Energizers and Icebreakers
4. Classic Management Games, Exercises, Energizers and Icebreakers (Volume 2)
5. Stress? No Way!! (Handbook on Stress Management)
6. *HSoftware* (Shyam Bhatawdekar's Effectiveness Model)
7. Competencies and Competency Matrix
8. Soft Skills You Can't Do Without (Goal Setting, Time Management, Assertiveness and Anger Management)
9. Essentials of Work Study (Method Study and Work Measurement)
10. Essentials of Time Management (Taking Control of Your Life)
11. Essentials of 5S Housekeeping
12. Essentials of Quality Circles
13. Essentials of Goal Setting
14. Essentials of Anger Management
15. Essentials of Assertive Behavior
16. Essentials of Performance Management & Performance Appraisal
17. Health Essentials (Health Is Wealth)
18. The Romance of Intimacy (How to Enhance Intimacy in a Relationship?)
19. Good People: *Novel, a refreshingly different love story*
20. Funny (and Not So Funny) Short Stories
21. Stories Children Will Love (Volume 1: Bhanu-Shanu-Kaju-Biju and Dholu Ram Gadbad Singh)
22. Travelogue: Scandinavia, Russia

To Our Family

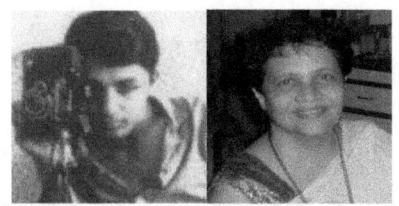

Shyam Bhatawdekar   Dr Kalpana Bhatawdekar

Do you feel less confident when you deal with others? Do you succumb to others' demands and do things that you do not wish to do? Do you want to be on equal footing with others but keep feeling otherwise? Do you end up shouting and getting angry with others to be on par with them? Have you become habitual of always proving your superiority to others by being aggressive? Is something wrong the way you approach people?

If answers to above-mentioned questions are "yes" then it makes a strong case for being "assertive" rather than continuing the existing submissive or aggressive behavior.

Therefore a thorough knowledge of "Assertive Behavior" becomes imperative. To facilitate gaining the knowledge in this vital subject in the shortest time, authors Shyam Bhatawdekar and Dr Kalpana Bhatawdekar included only the "essentials" of "Assertive Behavior" in the book.

The authors are top-notch business executives, successful entrepreneurs, highly sought after business and management consultants, eminent management gurus and scholars, authentic human behavior experts and prolific authors. And so the book becomes an authentic document on the subject.

To read more by the authors, refer their websites: http://shyam.bhatawdekar.com, *http://writings-of-shyam.blogspot.com* and http://management-universe.blogspot.com

Essentials of Assertive Behavior

Shyam Bhatawdekar
Dr Kalpana Bhatawdekar

Published by Publishing Division of

Prodcons Group

8, Pranjal Society, Shiv Tirth Nagar, Paud Road, Pune
411038 (India)

Email: prodcons@prodcons.com

For other web publications, refer: http://management-universe.blogspot.com and
http://shyam.bhatawdekar.com

Contents

Essentials of Assertive Behavior

Types of Behavior

Human behavior has remained an enigma over the ages. And therefore, it has been the subject of great studies by the learned pundits. They have tried to study and classify the behavior of human beings in various ways. Here in this book we are presenting the human behavior as classified in four different categories as given below. Won't it be interesting to know the category you belong to? Will you like to examine your own behavior pattern with reference to these? Then read the following descriptions under each of the four classifications and decide where you stand.

Passive (Submissive) Behavior: You shy away from or give up your rights, honest feelings, thoughts and beliefs. You do not express them at all and if you do, you do not express them unhesitatingly. You subordinate or even sacrifice your needs to someone else's needs particularly when the two needs conflict. You feel helpless, anxious, resentful and disappointed with self. You try to please others or avoid upsetting others because you fear them or fear hurting their feelings. You feel being manipulated and pushed around all the time.

Aggressive Behavior: You behavior is unfriendly and forceful. Your attacking behavior comes out as a result of being provoked and even without it. You generally dominate, forcing others to lose, show strength, are tense and achieve your ends at the cost of your and others' happiness. Your intention is to maintain dominance over the others; not worrying over the harm it may cause them. You are likely to feel angry and even frustrated, most of the time.

Passive-Aggressive Behavior (Indirect Aggression): As the name suggests the passive-aggressive style combines elements of both, the passive and aggressive styles. The anger of the aggressive style and the fear of the passive, both have the influence. The anger makes you want to "get" the other person but the fear holds you back from doing it directly. Therefore, you express aggression in subtle ways. When you are passive-aggressive, you disguise your aggression so that you can avoid taking responsibility for it. So you demonstrate practiced and pretentious helplessness, stubbornness, resentment, moods,

10

possibility of failure and even humor to shirk the tasks you are responsible for.

Assertive Behavior: You are capable of standing up for your personal rights and expressing your thoughts, feelings and beliefs in a direct, honest, confident and helpful way that do not aggressively violate the rights of others or submissively allow others to deny you your own rights. After expressing your thoughts and feelings you feel much better and your self-esteem goes up. You care for your self-respect and yet do not disrespect the others. Your behavior is neither aggressive nor submissive. You do not suffer from anxiousness under stress.

(When you try to introspect yourself with reference to the above-mentioned behavior patterns, you may find that you have shades of more than one behavior pattern. In such a case be guided by your dominant behavior pattern and that's where you belong at present).

In the following paragraph we are elaborating on the characteristics of the above-mentioned four behavior patterns to get a still clearer picture of these.

More on Characteristics of Behavior Patterns

Passive (Submissive) Behavior

People of passive behavior display the following characteristics:

- They don't like to displease or upset others. They will not tell the other persons the facts or ask/request to carryout things that they think will upset them.
- They can't easily say "no" and invariably yield to saying "yes" to others.
- In effect they may end up accepting the tasks, responsibilities and deadlines that are unachievable and difficult for them and as a result feel exploited and frustrated. They get bullied easily with a wishful thinking of becoming stronger.
- Even if they do not like the opinions or thinking of others they toe the line and cannot voice their own opinions and thoughts.
- They remain silent in the meetings or group discussions and do not put forth their ideas even if their ideas are brilliant.

- They have tendency of feeling inferior to others.
- They play a lose-win game (I lose, you win).

Other persons often ignore people with passive behavior. The passive behavior may also lead to serious internal conflict. The internal conflict in turn will generate stresses and strains, resentment and anger, feeling of being used and abused, feeling of getting exploited and victimized, desire to get even with or take revenge on those who have been aggressive.

Aggressive Behavior

People of aggressive behavior display the following characteristics:

- They bully others. They dominate over others. They yell and shout. They may even insult others. They may be even physically threatening.
- They force their opinions and thinking on others without giving any leeway to others. They belittle others' opinions and thinking.
- They flaunt their authority/status.
- They treat others with condescending manner.

- They have a tendency of feeling superior to others.
- They do not like being argued or questioned and even ask others to shut up. They are poor listeners. They interrupt others.
- They play a win-lose game (I win, you lose).

Aggressive behavior may seem to get you the things you want once in a while because of your aggression but in majority of dealings it will not work. Due to your constant aggression, your relationship with others will become unpalatable, mutual respect and trust will deplete and good number of people will start resenting you and avoiding you. You may end up having more enemies than friends.

Passive-Aggressive Behavior (Indirect Aggression)

People of passive-aggressive behavior display the following characteristics:

- They express their negative feelings indirectly rather addressing them openly.
- They do not say "no" to others' demand on them, may rather seem to agree (even enthusiastically) but actually resent and oppose them indirectly by

making excuses, procrastinating, screwing up the deadlines and even sabotaging.

- They say something but do something else.
- They cannot call spade a spade but will camouflage their true feelings (negative or positive) and speak out in an agreeable tone that aligns well with the expectations of the other person.
- When they wish to show anger or resentment towards the other persons, they will do so by keeping silent, telling lies, leading astray, sulking, mumbling, slamming the objects etc but will refuse to talk about the matter that annoyed them.
- Inwardly they have a tendency of feeling superior to others but outwardly (and to an onlooker) they demonstrate their inferiority.
- They play a double game- apparently a lose-win game (I lose, you win) but inherently a win-lose (I win, you lose) game.

Passive-aggressive behavior will make you into an undependable person. You relationships with others will suffer. Mutual respect and trust will also deplete. They can see your double game and they will keep away from you.

Assertive Behavior

People of assertive behavior display the following characteristics:

- They are clear about the objectives of their thinking, communication and actions. Therefore they start with the end in mind and roll out their dealings with others in a very streamlined manner.
- They express their feelings, ideas, dissents and needs without any fear or emotional overtures like anger, remorse etc.
- They speak out their mind in a balanced way without being aggressive, submissive or submissively aggressive.
- They can always communicate and act the way they wish to communicate and act but without emotionally, intellectually or physically belittling, disrespecting or hurting others and self.
- They can negotiate at par with others with an aim of reaching some mutually agreeable conclusions and solutions. They are quite flexible.
- They do not feel superior or inferior to others.

- They can initiate and maintain comfortable relationships with others.
- Their disposition is that of a confident person with necessary self-worth or self-esteem.
- They play a win-win game (I win, you win).

Assertive behavior pattern has hardly any drawback that other behavior patterns have. On the other hand it has many benefits. Assertive people can relate, communicate and negotiate with others quite comfortably. Despite putting forth their thoughts and feelings assertively they will be able to maintain honest and mutually respectful relationships with the people. Above all they carry great self-worth and an expression of "being".

What's Your Choice?

Now it's time to make a choice to adopt a behavior pattern. Having studied the characteristics of the four behavior patterns it seems pretty obvious that assertive behavior pattern should become your dominant behavior pattern.

If you do not belong to this category of behavior already, then you may like to train yourself in assertive behavior and practice it as your new behavior. You may not be able to become assertive overnight but with constant learning and practice you will definitely turn assertive gradually.

It is the only behavior that is capable of giving you higher, overall and long-term effectiveness. It also enables you to hold you head high and feel independent or on par with others in a scenario of interdependence. It is also the expression of being.

Assertiveness: The Expression of Being

- Assertiveness is the self-expression through which one stands up for one's own basic human rights without violating the basic rights of others.
- All of us should insist on being treated fairly. We have to stand up for our rights without violation of the rights of others.
- This means tactfully, justly and effectively expressing our preferences, needs, opinions and feelings.
- Being assertive is distinguished from being unassertive (weak, passive, compliant, self-

sacrificing) or aggressive (self-centered, inconsiderate, hostile, arrogant, demanding).

Why Assertiveness? (The Purpose)

- To speak up, make requests, ask for favors and generally insist that your rights be respected as a significant, equal human being.
- To overcome the fears and self-deprecation from those who keep you from exercising your rights.
- To express negative emotions (complaints, resentment, criticism, disagreement, intimidation, the desire to be left alone).
- To refuse requests if you wish to.
- To show positive emotions (joy, pride, liking some one, attraction).
- To give compliments.
- To accept compliments with "thank you".
- To ask why and question authority or tradition. Not to rebel but to assume responsibility, to take control of the situation and to make things better. You are not a slave.
- To initiate, carry on, change and terminate conversations comfortably.

- Share your feelings, opinions and expressions with others.
- To deal with minor irritations before your anger turns into intense resentment and aggression.

Assertive Rights

You must recognize your rights and stand up for them. If you do not, other people will define your role for you and you stop being yourself. Given below are your fair rights and these are often opposite of the mistaken traditional behavior expected of the people in general:

- You have the right to be treated with respect.
- You have the right to be treated as a human being equal to others in every way.
- You have the right to stand up for your rights and attain those rights.
- You have the right to do anything as long as it does not hurt someone else or your own self.
- You have the right to express your own feelings, opinions and convictions.
- You have the right to protest against unfair criticism and dealings.

- You have the right to put your needs and wants ahead of those of others if you wish to choose to do so for your own valid reasons.
- You have the right to maintain your dignity by being properly assertive even if hurts someone else, as long as your motive is assertive, not aggressive.
- You have the right to judge your own behavior, thoughts and emotions and to take the responsibility for their initiation and consequences upon yourself.
- You have the right to offer no reasons or excuses for justifying your behavior.
- You have the right not to apologize for everything that goes wrong.
- You have the right not to take the responsibility of others' problems.
- You have the right to judge if you take up responsibility for finding solutions to other people's problems.
- You have right to change your mind.
- You have the right to propose changes and negotiate with others to effect changes for the better.
- You have right to make mistakes, be responsible for them and correct them.
- You have right to say, "I don't know".

- You have the right to be independent of the goodwill of others before coping with them.
- You have the right to deal with others without being dependent on them for approval.
- You have the right to be illogical (and yet responsible to others and self) in making decisions.
- You have the right to say, "I don't understand."
- You have the right to clarify in case of doubts.
- You have the right to be listened to.
- You have the right to ask for more information. For this if necessary you have the right to interrupt others to seek clarifications.
- You have the right to say, "I don't care or I care."
- You have the right to say "no" without feeling guilty. You also have the right to say "yes".
- You have the right to set your own priorities.
- You have the right to pamper yourself.
- You have the right to feel and express your anguish or pain if you desire to do so.
- You have the right to ask for what you want.
- You have the right to request for support and help.
- You have the right to get what you pay for.
- You have the right to answer honestly when you are asked if you like something and you don't.

- You have the right to refuse to entertain a friend of your spouse whom you don't like.

- You have the right to be alone when you want to remain alone even though others are desirous of your company.

- You have the right not to necessarily accept others' advices.

- You have the right to make request of another person as long as you realize the other person has the right to say "no".

- You have the right not to act assertive when you choose to do so.

Now having known such a great deal of stuff on the need to develop the assertive behavior, we should find out how to learn and imbibe it.

Simple Assertiveness Tips and Techniques

We give below some simple and practical tips and techniques of becoming assertive. Read them carefully and start putting them into practice. You know the expression "practice makes a man (and woman) perfect".

1. Assess your existing behavior pattern

Introspect yourself and get to know your existing behavior pattern. If you are already assertive, you may still go through the following tips and techniques, use them and further strengthen your assertiveness. If you find yourself wanting in assertiveness, you definitely need to understand all the tips and techniques we are giving here and implement them.

Implementation is very important, only knowing them will not do. Initial hesitation will peter out gradually as you start practicing.

2. Scripting

The three-line assertion technique (called "scripting") as explained below is a very useful technique to assert yourself. It consists of the following three steps of delivering your assertive message:

1. *The facts of the event:* Understand the facts of the situation and summarize them.

2. *Your feelings:* Indicate your feelings towards the situation.

3. *Your need and resultant benefits:* State your requirements, reasons and benefits to the other party, if appropriate.

This technique enables you to confront the other person with your concern without being personally aggressive. It requires skillful conversation control and practice.

Example of the format:

You may say:

1. "When you............" (State facts)
2. "I feel uncomfortable............" (State feelings)
3. "I would like............" (State requirements). "In this way we will be able to work together more productively because............" (State benefits to the other party)

In extreme case, there can be a fourth line indicating the consequences of other person still not mending his ways.

25

You may say:

4. If you don't, I will………..

Let us take a concrete example from a real life situation now and see how we can script the assertive behavior.

Example:

A female employee to her male boss:

"In our departmental meetings where male folks are in majority, often dirty jokes, crude remarks aiming at the female employees and four letter/F words are exchanged freely. I have observed it over the last five meetings and noted it down. I feel very uncomfortable attending these meetings due to these happenings. You being the boss and chairman of these meetings, I will like you to impose a check on such behavior of our employees. This will bring in decorum and I will stop feeling sexually harassed."

In the above-mentioned script, we have used the three-statement technique and it should work. However if the boss of the department does not take action despite it, the female employee can use the fourth statement as follows:

"Despite my earlier two requests the use of dirty jokes, crude remarks towards the female employees and four letter/F words have continued in the departmental meetings unabated. If it does not stop in the next meeting onward I will have no other recourse but to report this sexual harassment to our HR department."

3. Rehearse Your Lines

Prior to confronting tricky and challenging situations, it will be a good idea to visualize the possible scenarios, decide on what you want for yourself and prepare what and how you will like to say it.

You may like to write down your lines and then practice speaking them aloud. If needed, rehearse a role-play with one of your confidants and elicit candid feedback.

If you do not find a person who can act as your sounding board, you can stand in front of a mirror and rehearse.

4. I statements

To lay emphasis and to assert yourself, you should use expressions like "I think", "I feel", "I need", "I want", "I expect", "I disagree" (rather than saying you are wrong) etc in your communication with others.

Examples: "Mommy, I want eggs in my breakfast daily now on." "I feel strongly that you should stop complaining about small things and start working." "I need to have your reply by tomorrow." "I expect you to be punctual now onward." "I disagree with your opinion that age must always be respected." "Please take the tea away right now. I want it when I have eaten my omelet."

5. Broken record

The name for this technique has its origin from the gramophone (vinyl) records of olden times. When a vinyl record suffered a scratch in its musical grooves, the gramophone needle would get stuck in the scratched portion and play that tiny segment of music or song over and over again.

So the essence of the broken record assertiveness technique is repetition of your requirements.

Particularly this technique can be used when the other person with whom you are dealing resists you or puts a brake on your requirements. Then despite resistance stick to your point. Keep repeating what you want or what you want to refuse. But do not show anger, helplessness, frustration, irritation, aggressiveness or any such emotions while making your point.

If your opponent is equally assertive or aggressive, the strength or impact of your successive repetitions may keep reducing to the extent that you may lose ground. Under such an eventuality you must keep some sanctions ready with you that you can open up at an appropriate time to press your demand.

Example 1:

Life Insurance Agent: I am presenting the most advantageous policy any insurance company has conceived so far.

Customer: I am not interested in any policy.

Agent: It has the features of flexi payment amounts and flexi periods of payment that provide you immense flexibility. No other policy as of date has such flexi features.

Customer: No, I am not interested in any policy.

Agent: Let me make you a quick presentation on how the policy works for you and your family and how your investment will bring in the maximum ever heard of returns. Sir, my since request is not to miss it.

Customer: No, I am not interested in any policy. Thanks.

Example 2:

Client: You have accepted this assignment and we want you to start on this assignment next week beginning.

Consultant: As discussed earlier the earliest I can start on it is after three weeks. Until then I am already committed.

Client: But this is extremely urgent project for us and it is essential that we start off immediately.

Consultant: I appreciate your urgency. But I must complete my prior commitments. I can take up yours after three weeks soon after I finish with my existing client.

Client: But for us that will be too late. We still insist the start date to be the next week.

Consultant: I am sorry but I will take up your assignment exactly after three weeks from now.

6. Say "no" when necessary

Many people find it very difficult to turn down any request coming from every nook and cranny. If you keep on accepting every request and demand you will be heavily burdened with tasks that you should not do in the first place and secondly it is not feasible to do all the tasks of the world. Learn to say "no" when you do not want to take up a demand or request made on you. Be direct. Say "No, I can't take it up till the next weekend." Or "No, I am afraid I can't do that." Or "I can't receive you at the airport this time. So please hire a taxi to reach my home."

You are not obliged to always give reason(s) to turn down a request. However in some cases you may find it appropriate to offer some explanation. No harm doing that. But keep it brief.

7. Fogging

You may like to use this technique when facing any criticism. The first thing you must remember is not to contest the criticism. Also do not counterattack. Rather you should adopt the following responses:

- Find if any part of the criticism is correct. Then agree with that part of the criticism.
- Find if the entire criticism is truthful. Then agree with it fully.
- At times, if appropriate, request more specific criticism. This is called negative inquiry.
- If you agree with your negatives, accept it by saying "I agree" or "Yes, that makes sense". This is called

negative assertion. But make sure to accept your criticism without letting up your demand.

- Workout a mutually agreeable solution.

8. Empathic Assertiveness

First principle of assertiveness is being firm. Yet depending upon the situation, you can also be empathic with the person you are dealing with. Putting yourself in other person's shoes and acknowledging his/her difficulty or compulsions will soften the way through the person and you may be able to get the things done your way. Make sure that your empathy towards the other person is seen and felt as a genuine empathy and not a mere pretention.

Example: Boss to subordinate: "I understand your concerns on working with the same person again with whom you had serious interpersonal problems earlier. If I were in your position I would have similar hesitations. Nonetheless this person's involvement in the proposed project is vital and two of you will need to work it out together. I will facilitate your working together. Why not three of us meet this evening and talk it over?"

9. Use confident body language

Many times your body language speaks a lot more than what you say. Therefore to make the first confident and assertive move, don the correct body language.

Stand upright, walk smartly and easily (not too erect nor too slouchy nor too lazily) while entering a room. Always sit upright without crossing your legs or folding your arms or wringing your hands. Maintain eye contact with the person you are communicating with. Resort to active listening by getting into a dialogue and avoiding monologue or being a passive listener. Your pace and tone of talking play an important role in maintaining assertive communication. You should not mumble and should be loud enough to be easily audible.

10. Do not lose control over your emotions

Getting emotional is natural. Yet, if you want to get a handle on being assertive you will need to learn to keep a check on your emotions particularly those that show you as submissive and aggressive person. Some examples of such emotions are crying, shedding tears, frustration, helplessness, whining, anger etc.

If you feel quite emotional tackling a particular situation, you will have to postpone confronting it. In the mean time you will have to calm down, look at the situation with a rational mind, work out the facts and then proceed. At times you may have to rehearse your part of the communication by using firm and level voice.

In such situations ask for more time. You may frankly tell the other person that you need more time and specify how much more time you need.

11. Escalation

At times your initial efforts may not bring the desired results. In such a case, in your successive efforts your stance should get tougher and tougher and your voice firmer and firmer without losing control over your emotions. The other person may yield or provide a satisfactory solution. However if it does not happen that way, you will need to pursue the matter with the same or higher level of firmness and you will have to tell the person what you next step will be in case a satisfactory solution is not reached. If even this approach proves unsuccessful you can warn this person that you will now take up the matter with his higher-ups and you will report to his boss the unsatisfactory dealings you suffered prior to escalating the matter.

Train Yourself on Being Assertive

Given below are some training exercises that you can do on your own in order to develop and further enhance your assertiveness.

Behavior Assignments: Impersonal Situations

1. Stop two or three people on street and ask for directions.

2. In a store ask for a few specific items not on display.

3. Go to three stores. In each, try an article- jacket, dress, shoes, belt, sunglasses, cap etc- but do not buy anything. This trains you on your right to reject or to say "no". If you fancy something you really want to purchase, go back later.

4. Go to two stores where you are not known and ask for change of $50 (or whatever is your currency and whatever amount you think is appropriate for this exercise). Don't buy anything. The next week ask for change of $100 and the third week for change of $500. Remember you do not have to get the change. Just ask. It the proprietor/cashier gives it to you, thank him. If he doesn't, say a polite, "Thanks, anyway."

5. Vary the "demand" technique of point no 4 above. Go to a newsstand where you are not known, take out a $10 note (or whatever is your currency and whatever amount you think is appropriate for this exercise) and ask for a newspaper. Do this twice or thrice the first week. The second week try it couple of times again but with higher denominations like $20 or $50. Make your request look like a matter of normal purchase. Do not hesitate or mumble any apology. The essence of doing it is just carrying out the exercise and training yourself in assertiveness and nothing else. Remember, you are not forcing the newspaper vendor to do anything and he or she also has the right to say "no".

6. Go to a restaurant where you are not known. Do not pick a time when there is too much of a rush of customers. Ask,

"May I have a glass of water please?" If you get it, drink down the water and express your thanks. If you don't get it, say, "Thanks, anyway" and leave.

7. Go to a coffee shop with a friend. Buy just one coffee. Request an extra empty cup. Share the coffee with you friend.

8. Buy something at a store with deliberate intention of returning it with no apology or explanation. Just say, "I would like to return this" to the salesperson. The intent of this task is to be able to return things without being or feeling apologetic about it.

9. Buy a few things in a store that you need to buy. Go to the cashier to pay and request for a discount. You may or may not present a reason for requesting the discount. If you get the discount, it's your gain. If you don't, choose between buying without the discount or walk away from the store without buying.

In carrying out the above-mentioned assignments:

1. Set a deadline.

2. Share the assignment with your spouse or your confidant so you know you will have to report to someone.

3. If you don't do an assignment for two consecutive weeks or so, you can safely conclude that the assignment made you pretty nervous. So take up any other assignment for the time being but do return to the assignment that created nervousness in you.

4. Go back and repeat the assignment again and again. This gives you the feeling of being in control.

Behavioral Assignments: Social Interactions

1. Say "good morning" to people at work. Don't expect a response. Any response you get is a bonus.

2. If you live in a township/community or in an apartment building, try saying "good morning" and "good evening" to fellow residents. You may even try greeting the passers-by on the street.

3. Without expecting a response, make comments to or strike a conversation with the person sitting next to you at the bus stop, in the train or the airplane etc. Your remarks could be as simple as, "Isn't it a nice day?"... "I think the

train is running late"... "Won't the bus ever come?"... "What's your experience of this airliner, I am flying this particular one the first time?"

4. Practice the expression of feeling. Look for opportunities to pay a compliment to a waiter, store clerk, co-worker, friend, spouse, your children, boss. Count the number of times you accomplish this in one week and double the frequency the next week and subsequent weeks.

5. In the same way, search out opportunity to express displeasure or annoyance to a waiter, store clerk, co-worker, friend, spouse, your children, boss. When the occasion comes up, you might say to the waiter, "This coffee is cold. Would you mind getting me hot coffee?" You can say to your child or spouse, "Will you please stop talking aloud? I am on a conference call." Or assert with your cell phone provider, "If I get this kind of bad service again, I am going to discontinue."

6. Tell your confidant or spouse something personal about yourself that you have never told anyone before. Of course share only such things that will not make you vulnerable.

7. Make it your business to do one task a week that you've wanted to do but have been putting off. It may be writing a letter or email to your old friend or telephone him/her, throw a small party to your friends or office colleagues.

Talk Your Feelings Assignment

Some people speak out what they think but not necessarily what they feel. Others cannot give spontaneous expression to their feelings or emotions. Some individuals fail to articulate their emotions altogether. And there are others who aren't even sure of their feelings. In a way all such people lack assertiveness in terms of giving ready expressions to their emotions. Remember, assertiveness is also the spontaneous experience and expression of feelings. Here is an exercise to develop this.

1. Plan to use the following three pairs of phrases as often as you can:

"I like what you said" ………..."I don't like what you said".
"I like what you did" ………….."I don't like what you did".
"I want you to……" …………"I don't want you to……..".

2. Make a chart in a tabular form with a space for each day of the week. At the end of each day, count the number of times you have used any of the six phrases. At the end of the week, total your count. Do this exercise for three or four successive weeks.

3. Monitor your use of the six phrases during the first week, then deliberately increase the number of times you say them during the second week and still more in the third and fourth weeks.

4. There is no harm continuing this exercise even beyond four weeks. Soon it will become your habit and there won't be any need to deliberately monitor it.

No One Is Born Assertive

The environmental factors and the way a person learns to think, feel and act under various situations often shape his behavior. A person is not born submissive, aggressive or assertive genetically. If at all we accept some genetic determinism, it plays much less role than the environmental impact on the person and his reaction/response to it.

Therefore, it is safe to say that human behavior is a learned phenomenon. And so the way it is learned, the same way a particular behavior pattern can be unlearned too. And in its place a new behavior can be learned and practiced.

That's why the persons who at present fall in the categories of submissive, aggressive or passive-aggressive behavior need not have to worry. They can learn and become assertive over a period of time if they follow the tips and techniques given in this book and also undertake the training exercises suggested in the book. Do not worry about making mistakes. "What if I make a mistake" is a barrier to assertion.